DANGEROUS
A GO-TO GUIDE FOR CHURCH COMMUNICATION

EDITED BY KEVIN D. HENDRICKS, CLEVE PERSINGER, & CHUCK SCOGGINS

Published by the Center for Church Communication
Los Angeles, California
www.CFCCLabs.org

Copyright © 2013 Center for Church Communication
Except "4 Mistakes From My First 3 Years as a Communications Director" and "7 Reasons You're Not Getting a Stage Announcement" Copyright © 2013 Phil Bowdle, used by permission; "3 Secret Questions" Copyright © 2012 Eric Murrell, used by permission; and "7 Things Every Church Facebook Expert Should Know" Copyright © 2013 Cleve Persinger, used by permission.

Cover design by Laura Bennett
Layout by 374 Designs

All rights reserved. No part of this book may be used or reproduced in any manner whatsoever without permission, except in the case of brief quotations.

To all the spouses, family and friends who help make Creative Missions possible. Know how important your support is. Lives are being changed because of the week you give up, too.

TABLE OF CONTENTS

Foreword by Cleve Persinger 1
3 Secret Questions by Eric Murrell 5
Little Guys Can Do Big Things Too by Kevin D. Hendricks 8
5-Minute Church Communication Strategy by Joe Porter 12
How to Do a Communications Self-Audit
by Danielle Hartland 15
What's Your Story by Kevin D. Hendricks 19
5 Ways to Do Church Communication on the Cheap
by Joe Porter 22
The Forgotten Few Minutes Before Church by Kim Fukai 26
7 Reasons Why You're Not Getting a Stage Announcement
by Phil Bowdle 29
Church Design Basics by Laura Bennett 32
How to Choose a Printing Company by Chuck Scoggins 36
How to Do Video on a Budget by Dave Hartland 40
Simple Tweaks to Improve Your Sound System
by Colt Melrose 45
How to Write Church Announcements by Kelvin Co 48
Top 5 Elements for a Church Site by Matt Adams 51
How to Find a Web Company for Your Church
by Matt Adams 54
Getting Organized With Google by Evan Courtney 57
Getting Your Church Started With Facebook
by Matt Adams 62
7 Things Every Church Facebook Expert Should Know
by Cleve Persinger 65
**4 Mistakes From My First 3 Years as a Communications
Director** by Phil Bowdle 70
Need More? 74
About the Center for Church Communication 75
About Creative Missions 78
Acknowledgments 81

FOREWORD
BY CLEVE PERSINGER

It took only a week to make Pastor Jeff dangerous.

A team of church creative professionals from around the country had descended on his church to help tackle communication projects. We call it Creative Missions and by the end of that first trip in 2011, Pastor Jeff and his church were empowered to communicate the message of the gospel.

Now they could accomplish anything. They were dangerous.

An Idea Is Born

Only a year before that first trip I published a blog post sharing the vision God had given me for Creative Missions. I'd served on many mission trips, in multiple roles, but I continually felt I could be of greater help by using the gifts God had given me. I thought maybe I could contribute more using my communication knowledge than my sub-par painting skills. So I asked, "As a creative on short-term mission trips, do you ever feel like you could be serving more through the talents and abilities God has blessed you with?" We were overwhelmed by the response from creatives and techies alike. It's still the most popular post I've ever written.

Every year Creative Missions pairs teams of communication and tech gurus with 15 to 20 under-resourced churches and ministries in a target region to create sustainable solutions and strategies that engage. We help these churches tell the greatest story ever told.

With several successful trips now behind us, we've seen God do amazing things. With logos, websites, social media, signage, videos and sound system optimizations—just to name a few—churches are able to communicate the gospel to their communities in new ways and with renewed zeal.

They've become dangerous.

The Stories

"We've seen more impact in more churches helping us engage our region with the gospel in that one week than at any other time before," the director of a network of churches we served in Albany, N.Y., told us.

Creative Missions is completing tasks that have been weighing pastors and churches down, sometimes for years. Burdens are removed and spirits are restored. We've seen real tears. It's usually a lack of resources, bandwidth or expertise that's holding these churches back.

"This week has lifted a huge weight off my shoulders as a lead pastor," said Pastor Andy from Rogers, Ark. "The work accomplished allows us to focus more on getting Jesus to Northwest Arkansas!"

We've been encouraged by stories from folks at their wit's end, just about to abandon the work to which God has called them. One elder board said, "Your timing couldn't be more perfect," sharing they were just about to shut their church's doors. The toughest-looking guy at the table stood up with tears in his eyes and said, "God brought us this far—we don't want to stop."

Over a year later, I'm happy to say (and the elders were happy to report) they don't even look like the same church we originally met. Volunteers have stepped up to help with various communication and tech needs. Folks are hearing the gospel like never before, and God is changing lives.

You're Not Alone

These churches have become dangerous. They're effectively sharing the good news and making a difference in their communities. They've endangered the status quo. They've threatened the idea that church has become irrelevant. They're a danger to the "that's how we've always done it," mentality that cripples so many churches. All because they got some help.

Is your church ready to be dangerous? We're ready to help.

The following pages have been written by men and women who are in the trenches of church communication. The reinforcements. They served on Creative Missions trips, helping under-resourced churches and ministries. They offer that same insight, wisdom and help to you. We can't travel to every church, but you are not alone.

"For the first time since we started pastoring, we don't feel alone," one husband-wife pastor team told us.

When we come together, we are strong.

When we raise our voice, we become dangerous.

When we serve our God, nothing can stop us.

As our society becomes increasingly visual and media-saturated, may we always be looking for better ways to communicate the gospel.

I pray you profit from the advice found in this book as kingdom workers have before you, and then pass it along to others in need.

Cleve Persinger helps churches engage community both online and off. He's the external communications strategist for The Chapel, a multi-site church in Chicagoland, and founder of MediaBLEEP and Creative Missions.

Web: MediaBLEEP.com
Twitter: @persinger

3 SECRET QUESTIONS
BY ERIC MURRELL

A lot of people want you to believe the basics of communication are tough to master. There are a lot of great books, consultants and classes, but the truth is: it's pretty easy to get started. You just have to know the right questions to ask.

Through Creative Missions and other projects, I've had a lot of time to fine tune a process to help ministries reboot their approach to general communication. The start of this process involves three "secret" questions that every ministry needs to ask. They may be simple, but they're surprisingly effective. Give them a shot:

1) Who are you?

Everyone always laughs at this question, but I've rarely met a ministry that can answer this in less than two sentences (my required length). It's a tough question, but it's something you need to answer. It sits at the core of everything you do as a church. Who are you? Really? What is your personality? Where do you want to take people?

The answer should be about two sentences long and should be easily understood by the average human (try to avoid theological language and business speak). Think of it as the "elevator pitch" for your ministry.

One of the best examples of this I've ever seen came from one of the pastors at The Awakening of Northwest

Arkansas (a church we served for Creative Missions 2012). After our team of "experts" put our heads together and suggested slogans for a few minutes, the pastor casually threw out this amazing mission statement: "We want our church to be a place where people can come to relax, worship and discover truth."

Wow... doesn't get much better than that!

2) Who are you trying to reach?

Another basic question, right? The gut-reaction, quick answer to this one is to immediately blurt out: "Everyone!"

While that is generally an accurate statement, it's not very helpful. Most ministries are called to a much more specific target. I like to create an imaginary person ("First Baptist Frank" or "Grace Church Gary") and use these questions to build out a persona:

- How old are they? What's their average life stage? (e.g., 30- to 40-year-old young families)
- What does their average day look like?
- What's their previous experience with Christianity? With church?
- What's their biggest felt need?
- What's their existing perception of us (both positive and negative)?

Having answers to these questions will give you a critical foundation that leads to my final question.

3) How are you communicating who you are to the people you're trying to reach?

You know who you are and who your audience is. Now, are you communicating to them in a way they actually get?

It's amazing how clarifying this question can be. A lot of times I find we are projecting our preferences onto an audience that needs a different approach. Maybe you're sending out an email newsletter to an audience that mostly engages with physical media. Maybe you're spending thousands of dollars on print with an audience that doesn't look past their iPad screen.

Use what you discover in this process to change the way you approach your community. I think you'll be surprised at the results.

> Eric Murrell is the communication manager at Long Hollow Baptist Church, a member of the Creative Missions leadership team, and the creator of the Prayer Engine and Series Engine plugins for WordPress. Eric and his wife Lauren reside in Hendersonville, Tenn., with their two children.

Web: EricMurrell.com
Twitter: @EricMurrell

LITTLE GUYS CAN DO BIG THINGS TOO

BY KEVIN D. HENDRICKS

I go to an Episcopal church. We have liturgy. Our pews aren't padded. We don't do PowerPoint. We don't have a visitor's welcome center. Our website? Not so flashy. Our communications budget? Nonexistent. A communications committee has started and failed multiple times in the last decade.

We're what you call a normal church. One of the little guys.

I say that so you understand I'm not from one of these cutting edge churches with communications directors and flat panel TVs and sermon graphics. We've got an admin assistant, and Janice puts together a mean newsletter.

So understand where I'm coming from when I say this: There's hope for the little guy.

When communication professionals start talking big plans, it's a little overwhelming for us little guys. They're debating microsites and we're still high-fiving that we even *have* a website.

But don't let that scare you away. Don't let that intimidate you.

The truth is you're already communicating. Don't let the fact that you're little stop you from making it better.

Here are some ways the little guy can step it up:

Make a Plan

Every time my church starts a new communications effort, whether it's a new website or a new logo, it gets mired down and mucked up. Why? Because we have no plan. Before you talk designs or even methods, start with the basics. Who are you? Why are you communicating? What are you going to say? Who does the work?

Baby Steps

We little guys are no megachurch. We're not ready to tweet and blog and podcast. So start small. Make one steady, consistent, maintainable improvement at a time. Baby steps to the website. Baby steps to bulletins without typos. Baby steps to ditching clipart. Aim for incremental improvements. Good communication is like a light guiding you in the darkness: It can't flare up and fade out, it has to burn slow and steady through the night.

Find a Champion

What we little guys really lack is dedicated people power. We have no staff. Janice is a rock star of an admin assistant, but her job description is six pages long. She makes the church run, she doesn't have time to moonlight as a communications director. So find champions. For each new project, find a champion who will love it, run with it and win. Show them the plan, give them some direction and empower them to make their own decisions (and their own mistakes).

Do Something
The biggest killer of progress is a lack of progress. If you don't get anywhere you'll discourage and dishearten your volunteers and you'll be starting over again. Adopt the mindset of a startup and do it quick and cheap. Make it better as you go, but make sure you're going. Don't wait for perfection.

Ignore the Dissent
We little guys invented "that's how we've always done it." Change is scary (try suggesting PowerPoint). So as your champion is getting something done with baby steps all according to plan, it's inevitable that someone will cry out "Facebook is the devil!" And now it's time to let the dissenters down easy. Change is a comin' and this little guy may be little, but he's going to communicate well. Don't let dissent grind you down.

See It In Action
I say all this because it works. My little church launched a new website last month. We did it with two very part-time volunteers in less than two months. The site isn't flashy, but it works. Rather than holding out for perfection, we launched it. Rather than waiting until we had copy for every ministry and perfect photos, we worked with what we had. Come up with a plan. Incremental improvements. Make progress. It's a strategy that can work no matter how small your church is.

Little Guys Can Do Big Things
So remember the story of Junior Asparagus in the VeggieTales version of David and Goliath: "He's big! But God's bigger! ... With his help little guys can do big things too!"

We may be small, but we're not out.

We may not be rock stars, but we can still sing.

We may be little guys, but we've got the same grand story.

And we can tell it well.

Kevin D. Hendricks is the editor of Church Marketing Sucks and editorial director for the Center for Church Communication. He's a freelance writer and editor in St. Paul, Minn., and likes to read a lot—he wrote *137 Books in One Year: How to Fall in Love With Reading*.

Web: KevinDHendricks.com
Twitter: @KevinHendricks

5-MINUTE CHURCH COMMUNICATION STRATEGY

BY JOE PORTER

Some will say that the very act of sitting down to come up with a communication strategy will improve how you communicate. While that may be true, it helps if you ask the right questions:

Question 1:
Who is my church trying to reach?

You might be tempted to say, "Everyone!", but start with your church's mission statement. Everything you do will trickle down from the mission of your church. If your church is like most churches, it probably has some sort of evangelistic phrase in its mission statement. In fact, if you asked your senior leaders to share their heart about who they would like to reach, they will most likely speak of reaching those who do not already know Jesus.

This step is critical because it will drive how you communicate in your bulletin, website and from the stage. It will force you to come up with a communication system that is easy, obvious and strategic. It means you give preference to the outsider who has not yet been to your church, as opposed to the insider who has been there for years.

Example: Every weekend at our church we have a short video program before the service that talks about things going on at the church. Over half of the content is for someone who is new or who is not yet involved. This means the person who is already involved continues to hear much of the same information every week. But it is critical to have a consistent message for a first timer to have a great first experience with your church. Everything must happen in balance, but if the mission of your church is to reach those not in the church then start talking to them!

Question 2:
How are we going to reach our audience on the weekend and during the week?

The weekend seems easy, but without a strategic plan it will turn to chaos. You will need to put together a simple criteria to determine what will be talked about through your bulletin, from the stage and on the screens. The easy criterion to start from is what percentage of your total audience does a particular announcement apply to. If it is below 80% then you might not want to talk about it from the stage. If it is below 50% then you might not want to talk about it at all on the weekends.

But don't stop there. Your website, email newsletter and social media should continue to engage and dialog about the same things that are talked about on the weekend. Your website should always be the most trusted source of information. Then all other media (Facebook, Twitter, Pinterest, etc.) should point to that content.

The most important element about reaching your online audience is engagement. Don't just tell them the information you want them to hear. Dialog with them. Ask questions. Post photos. Have fun!

By asking these two simple questions, you'll begin to frame a strategy from which to start. Focus on communicating creatively and effectively to the people already connected to your church to get them motivated, excited and equipped for outreach. Then you can begin to focus on external marketing based on your mission and budget.

> Joe Porter is the communications director at Whitewater Crossing in Ohio. He has a boisterous time with his wife and two kids while maintaining his photo/video business.

Web: InnovatoryProductions.com
Twitter: @InnovatoryPhoto

HOW TO DO A COMMUNICATIONS SELF-AUDIT

BY DANIELLE HARTLAND

Before we talk about how we should probably talk about why. Regular, scheduled, self-audits are important for a lot of reasons, but for our purposes I'm going to focus on three:

1. **Consistency:** Ministry is fast-paced. A lot of times, we are flying by the seat of our pants just to get the next email newsletter out. By the time six months have passed, the people around you have probably tried to get things done their own way (I lovingly call this "unintentional innovation"). In fact, you've probably made a few weird choices yourself. It's important to recalibrate and make sure everyone is on the same page.

2. **Vision Leaks:** If you can take time to look over what you're doing and get feedback, you'll be able to identify which part(s) of your vision needs to be re-communicated.

3. **Effectiveness:** Sometimes, we fall into the pattern of doing things because we've always done them (or because they're easy). If you can take an honest look at your methods, it will help you measure their effectiveness and make changes as needed.

Let's Get Auditing

Time for the "how." The first thing you need to do is take an assessment of everything you're currently doing. This is probably the hardest part, but it's the most foundational. Literally sit down and write out everything you do to communicate in your church. You might want to break it down by ministries and/or time frames. The list should be comprehensive, so be sure to take your time.

Once you have that list, you'll want to actually assess each item. Here are a few ways to accomplish that:

Surveys: Send out electronic and/or paper surveys to people in your congregation asking them about different communication methods. Use a very simple rating scale for each thing you mention:

> 0 = I have no idea what you're talking about.
>
> 1 = Never use it.
>
> 2 = I've seen it before, but it wasn't helpful.
>
> 3 = I could take it or leave it.
>
> 4 = I use this a lot (almost every time it's available).
>
> 5 = I fully rely on this to know what's happening.

Be sure not to overwhelm people: the less choices they have, the better. I'd suggest choosing no more than five things for people to rate. If it were me, for example, I would choose our website, weekly bulletin, email newsletter and Facebook posts.

Staff One-on-Ones: If you break your communication methods into ministry areas, it would be great to sit down with the leaders of that ministry and get their opinion on how it's going. Remember, this is a fact-finding mission to make your methods more effective and help you serve people better, it's not an opportunity to defend yourself. Hear the leaders out and learn from their perspectives.

Feedback Loops: Create a very short questionnaire for participants to complete after certain events/classes. It can be as simple as this:

How did you find out about _____?

What made you actually decide to come?

A communications self-audit is not something you'll be able to do constantly, so here are some strategic times to focus on getting input:

- After big events.
- With a new ministry launch.
- Before a web redesign.
- When vision initiatives change.

The only thing "self" about a communications self-audit is that you have to commit to it. Everything else about this process involves others. It is crucial to get opinions from the people who use, and hopefully benefit, from the methods you've come up with. If you want to get the most out of this experience, be open to criticism, change and new ideas. It will not only make your communication strategies better, it will make your relationships better and it will make you a better leader.

Danielle Hartland is the creative director at Grace Church in Erie, Pa., where her goal is to create and foster accessible communication strategies that cut through without cutting in, along with awesome gatherings and experiences.

Facebook: /DanielleSuzanne
Twitter: @DanielleSuzanne

WHAT'S YOUR STORY
BY KEVIN D. HENDRICKS

People don't come to church on Sunday morning for the announcements. Yet too often when churches communicate, all they focus on are the announcements. Our bulletins, newsletters, Facebook updates, blog posts and more are dominated by stories that, let's face it, don't matter.

Churches talk about a lot of stuff nobody cares about:

- We need more volunteers in the nursery.
- There's a clean up day on Saturday.
- Potluck next Sunday, bring a dish to share.

Sure, these things are important. You want capable volunteers caring for babies. Your building and grounds should be clean, safe and inviting. People need to know the practical details of a church-wide gathering.

But let's call these announcements what they are: Housekeeping.

Gospel vs. Housekeeping

There are important updates that need to be communicated. But they're not everything. Your church has the greatest story ever told. Are you telling that gospel story in your communications or are you talking about diapers in the nursery?

Realistically your communication will involve some housekeeping. You have to share announcements, events, times and dates. Not everything has to be holy. But the key is that those housekeeping items shouldn't dominate. There should still be a story that matters in the stream of updates.

If your church is here to tell people about Jesus, make sure that's the case in your communication. If housekeeping dominates your communication—you're doing it wrong. The story you're telling isn't the gospel, it's that your church is really busy doing stuff.

It's all housekeeping and no substance.

Communicate Substance

Give us something more:

- Don't just talk about what you do, but why you do it: Explain why you're collecting canned goods and share God's heart for the poor.
- Don't tell us what's going to happen, without telling us what happened: Tell the stories of how God moved at last week's event.
- Put people and their stories before events and their details. Stories are engaging. Don't just talk about reading the Bible, tell stories about how it changes people.
- Talk about benefits, not features. Features are just details, but benefits are why it matters.

Stories That Spread

Your communication is what lasts beyond Sunday. It's what your congregation takes home. It's one of the few things anyone outside your congregation will ever see.

Consider what someone in your congregation would share with a friend: Choir rehearsal times or a video of the choir performance?

Yes, your church communications need to include those housekeeping announcements. But nobody lives for housekeeping. Do more. Tell a story of substance. We've got the greatest story ever told. What story is your church telling?

Kevin D. Hendricks is the editor of Church Marketing Sucks and editorial director for the Center for Church Communication. He's a freelance writer and editor in St. Paul, Minn., and likes to read a lot—he wrote *137 Books in One Year: How to Fall in Love With Reading*.

Web: KevinDHendricks.com
Twitter: @KevinHendricks

5 WAYS TO DO CHURCH COMMUNICATION ON THE CHEAP

BY JOE PORTER

"If I had an unlimited communications budget, then I would _____."

I would make a pretty confident bet that no church has dedicated an unlimited amount of funds to communications. In fact, most of us operate on what we consider a limited budget. This means we have to get creative about communicating with excellence. Here are the five ways that I have been able to make my limited budget go as far as possible:

1. Dig on Vimeo for Promo Videos

If you are like me, you see the value in moving pictures behind your ad. But it is not practical to hire a production company every time you want to promote an event or initiative. And there is too much junk on YouTube. You might already be using Vimeo to host your videos, but did you know a lot of artists openly grant access and allow you to download videos for free? Search some keywords and be sure to check the box "downloadable." Boom. Then you can spend your money on design and editing. (Make sure you're only grabbing videos licensed for reuse. You can also set the search box to look for specific licensing. Also user beware, not every licensed video is fully licensed and good to go.)

2. Download Existing Designs for Marketing

It might surprise you to know how many large and growing churches use pre-existing designs, templates and other shared media. If you have a limited staff and budget, you probably should not be spending 10 hours working on a custom graphic for your men's banquet or hiring a designer to do it. An example of a website that facilitates this inexpensive design sharing: Creation-Swap (http://cmsucks.us/n3). Most graphics are free and can be downloaded as an original source file (i.e. Photoshop, Illustrator, etc.)

3. Target Market with Facebook Ads

If you are bummed that you don't have the budget to do a mail drop to the 20,000 people in your market, then this will comfort you. You can reach an exponentially larger and more targeted audience for much less money by harnessing the amazing power of Facebook ads. For example: We ran a simple five-day ad on Facebook to promote our Easter web page. It targeted those who are friends with someone already connected to our Facebook page (approximately 1,800 followers at the time) who also live within a 10-mile radius from our church.

The results?

- Total individuals who saw the ad at least once: 8,491
- Actions taken/clicks: 401
- Total spent: $38.58

That's like 401 people calling your church office after sending out 8,491 invite cards! There are so many great reports and articles out there that can get you started with Facebook advertising, so do some research and get started.

4. Piece Together a Web Presence

You might already know that your web presence needs refreshing. Maybe you need to start over. If you look for all-in-one packages like I did when I started out, then you'll probably be disappointed with the cost per month. While there are lots of advantages to this option (web hosting, design, forms, email, etc., included in one fee), you are usually stuck in an expensive contract with little or no expansion possibilities. Instead begin to make a list of all web functions you require, then set out to get them individually. Remember you are reading about church comm on the cheap, not the easy. Example:

- Web template/structure: WordPress
- Web hosting/support: Local web nerd
- Forms: Wufoo
- Sermon audio/video: Series Engine
- Video hosting: Vimeo
- Audio hosting: Dropbox
- Giving: PayPal
- Calendar: ServiceU
- Email: Google Apps

By piecing together services you also have the ability to adapt to growth or get rid of an area that is not working while retaining control of all the pieces.

5. Dirt Cheap Printing

You can print high-quality, full-color pieces for cheaper than you think. Web printers like UPrinting, VistaPrint,

ClubFlyers and others have very affordable prices. You can get 1,000 full-color, two-sided business cards for $25. Consider the possibilities of printing invite cards and doing a 'bring a friend' push for your next event.

Church communication doesn't have to be costly. This is just a quick sampling of ways you can promote your church without spending a lot of cash.

> Joe Porter is the communications director at Whitewater Crossing in Ohio. He has a boisterous time with his wife and two kids while maintaining his photo/video business.

Web: InnovatoryProductions.com
Twitter: @InnovatoryPhoto

THE FORGOTTEN FEW MINUTES BEFORE CHURCH

BY KIM FUKAI

It's Sunday morning. Your parking lot is covered—no one is getting inside without being safely directed to a parking spot. Your greeters all remind you of a hug from your grandmother—warm and a little bit squishy. And your ushers are kind of like your parking team, but they couldn't handle the extreme weather changes, so instead they guide people to a seat.

What happens in those few minutes after your visitors take their seat in the auditorium/sanctuary/worship center and before the service begins? I speak of visitors because, let's be honest, they're the ones who come early. Your regulars meander in because they know what to expect. It's easy to forget about those few minutes, yet they matter when lost people find themselves in a seat at your house.

Vibe. You know what I'm talking about. It's the never seen, but always felt energy. It's the groove you want everyone to feel. After all, you're about to ask them to engage for the next hour or more and you need a solid starting point. Vibe communicates a lot about your church. Vibe is found in the environment.

Your church's approach to this time needs to fit your values. Whatever your worship environment, here are some things to think about that will help you become more intentional about the vibe before your service starts:

Listen.
What do you want people hear? Maybe it's music fitting your worship style, silence for a reverent room or the buzz from people sharing their life stories with each other.

What potential distractions can be heard: A guitar tuning on stage, your pastor checking his microphone, kids running around the sanctuary?

See.
Where are people looking: Up at giant screens with well-presented announcements, down at their carefully laid out bulletin or handouts, out at their physical surroundings?

What could negatively impact some one's visual experience: A stage cluttered with cables and random personal items, lack of personal space in the seats, a banner that is frayed or about to fall off?

Feel.
Emotive and, at times, frustratingly subjective. So throw some adjectives out there! Joyful. Welcoming. Peaceful. Rockin'. What are you doing to express these things?

What could be felt in your room that takes away from this: Fear of the unknown, anxiety over what's expected, deep-seated guilt?

Improve the Vibe.
Listen, see and feel the vibe that visitors experience in those forgotten few minutes before your church service

starts. Once you're paying attention to that experience, you can start to improve it.

> Kim Fukai is the director of programming and production at Grace Point Church in San Antonio, Texas. As a member of Creative Missions 2012, she had an amazing experience coordinating the Creative Missions worship conference and serving local churches with the Tech Team.

Twitter: @KimFukai

7 REASONS WHY YOU'RE NOT GETTING A STAGE ANNOUNCEMENT

BY PHIL BOWDLE

One of the most challenging things in service planning for pastors and communication leaders can be managing stage announcements. Without a system and strategy in place, you can quickly find yourself stuck in a rhythm of wasting 10 minutes on announcements, while not being effective with any of them.

Time is limited and stage announcements are not the answer to everything. Here are seven reasons why you're not getting a stage announcement:

1. It doesn't apply to at least 80% of the audience.

This is the most important question you can ask when deciding if something should be announced from stage. I do occasionally break this 80% rule for key ministry on-ramp events/programs, or when it's a direct next step for what's being preached about in the sermon.

2. It should be announced at your ministry event, not the whole church.

For example, if you need to communicate an event happening with student ministry, the most effective place to get the word out is at your student ministry gatherings. Same applies to other areas.

3. There's no clear "why."

If you can't share the "why" associated with the announcement in less than 30 seconds, it's going to be hard to communicate effectively from the stage.

It's going to be even harder to get your audience to care.

4. The announcement sends them on a rabbit trail.

Is there childcare? Do I have to register? Where is the event? Without knowing the who, what, when, where, how and why of the announcement, you'll quickly create more questions than answers and lose your audience in the process. Effective announcements have a clear next step involved for what they should do next. It's OK to not mention every detail, but it's crucial to communicate where they can find all the info they need. For us at West Ridge, we always communicate that they can get more information at our Help Center in the atrium or at WestRidge.com. If it's announced on a Sunday, we include a link to that program/event on the home page so it's easy to find for our visitors.

5. It's not an effective time to announce it.

One of the keys to developing a communications plan is to be strategic about when you're going to promote programs and events. Don't waste bandwidth on announcing something before your audience can do anything with that information. For example, if you're announcing Christmas service times, it's more important to announce that in the two to three weeks before Christmas when your audience is making plans than it is in November when it's likely too far off to do anything with that information.

6. It's a bandage for a short-term problem, not part of an on-going strategy.

Do you need two more volunteers in the nursery? There are two ways you can approach this:

Option #1: Announce from stage that you need two more volunteers in the nursery. You'll likely find the volunteers, but you'll create a precedent for every ministry to ask for stage announcements any time they are a couple volunteers short. Also, your audience will think that the only place you need volunteers is in the nursery.

Option #2: You strategically and consistently announce to the whole audience that there are opportunities across the church to serve and make an impact. Finding these opportunities and getting plugged in should be simple. Now you're encouraging everyone to take their next step in serving and building your volunteer base across all ministries.

7. There are too many things being announced already.

If you really want your announcements to be effective, pick one or two announcements that are most important for your audience to know and say no to the rest.

Phil Bowdle is the communications director at West Ridge Church in Atlanta. You can follow along with his blog at PhilBowdle.com, which is focused on being a practical conversation and resource on church communications.

Web: PhilBowdle.com
Twitter: @PhilBowdle

CHURCH DESIGN BASICS
BY LAURA BENNETT

Each year on Creative Missions we meet with churches that have little knowledge of church communication, few resources to accomplish that communication or both little knowledge and few resources. I'm grateful I get to be a part of the design process for these churches. I'm blessed by the conversations we have with these pastors and volunteers on how effective communication pieces (and everything is a communication piece) help them reach their congregations and communities. Through those conversations, we end up exploring and creating branding and identity, sermon branding, and promotions and advertising.

Branding & Identity

Your church's brand is the visual representation of your identity, vision and mission. Meaning a church should have a clear vision of who they are and who they are trying to reach before even thinking of putting pen to paper on a logo or other design elements. So stop. Go do that before you read further. (Need help? We've talked a bit about brand and identity before.)

Ready? Good. When creating your church's look and feel, be current yet sustainable. Don't chase cool. Don't out-trend yourself. Once it's created and implemented, be consistent. Consistency tells people you are trustworthy and not flaky. I was a part of a church that had three different logos in two years. Were we going through an identity crisis? Yep.

Branding Resources: This isn't even a scratch on the surface of church branding. To go a little deeper, check out the book *Outspoken: Conversations on Church Communication* for more thoughts and practices. And here are some more helpful sites:

- 100 Principles for Designing Logos and Building Brands (http://cmsucks.us/n1)
- How to Rebrand: 19 Questions to Ask Before You Start (http://cmsucks.us/n2)

Sermon/Message Branding

Matt Papa, a worship leader at the Summit Church in Raleigh-Durham, N.C., says that a song is more than just lyrics and melody but it's a sermon for people to remember. I echo this on sermon and message branding. Pastors spend each week planning a message that hopefully proclaims truth and the gospel and then present that message each weekend. By creating a look for a sermon series, you can give people something to hold on to after the message. Sermon branding is the time to be edgy and trendy. Be intriguing and compelling. Go all out.

Sermon Branding Resources: Here are some sites that have free resources and inspiration for planning and creating the look of your next sermon series:

- CreationSwap (http://cmsucks.us/n3)
- Stuff I Can Use (http://cmsucks.us/n4)

Promotions & Advertising
(aka The Kitchen Sink)

As church communicators, we're responsible for getting the tedious details of every event, devotional, weekly meeting, pastors' blog and message to the masses. Sometimes this comes in the form of a bulletin, a webpage, an announcement screen, a tweet, etc. I call this "promotions"—anything you need to promote "inside" the church to the congregation. Then there is advertising—anything you want the community outside the church to know. This can come in the form of a billboard, Facebook ad, newspaper ad, flier, invite card, etc. In either case, designing something that is clear and attractive is a must.

But remember when everything is important, nothing is important. Choose what you promote and advertise wisely. Don't over design. The information on the page is still more important than the design. Help lead people through what you want them to know with the design. Don't hide the information in the design.

Marketing Resources: Eric Murrell wrote articles last year on internal marketing (http://cmsucks.us/n5) and external marketing (http://cmsucks.us/n6).

I hope this was helpful to anyone starting out in church communications. Design is a powerful tool and I believe God wants us to use our gifts for his glory and to partner with him in building his church.

Laura Bennett is a Georgia girl living in Chapel Hill, N.C., as a freelance graphic designer and communications consultant. She has served as communications director at The Fellowship (formerly Two Rivers Baptist Church) and is a Creative Missions alum.

Web: LauraBennett.me
Twitter: @LauraBennett113

HOW TO CHOOSE A PRINTING COMPANY

BY CHUCK SCOGGINS

One of the first big decisions I had to make when getting started in my first church communications job was selecting a printing company for the church. Prior to my arrival, they were using a quick print company and I felt pretty certain there had to be a better option. We were paying too much and had too few printing features to choose from with the quick printer.

So I set out to find a new printing partner, but I was clueless where to start. After years in church communications and after experiences with dozens of printing companies, I have a few tips that will hopefully help you if you find yourself in a similar search.

The first decision you need to make is whether to use an online printing company like GotPrint.com or OvernightPrints.com or a local company. There are benefits and disadvantages to both and you might find yourself switching back and forth depending on the project.

Online companies often do a higher quantity and have less overhead, so generally you can find a better price. Also, they usually have the latest equipment and offer easy methods of file delivery (usually an online upload and proofing tool). However, if you want to see a physical proof, you are out of luck with an online printer. There are also the issues of longer turn-around times and extra costs associated with shipping.

Local printing companies also tend to offer a little better personal customer service. There is something nice about being able to pick up the phone and call someone if you have a question about color matching, paper weight or imposing.

For me, I never liked the thought of being just another customer and I certainly viewed my printing company as a partner in ministry. It was a blessing to be able to minister to the owner of a printing company I once worked with by visiting him in the hospital after his cancer surgery. It is those relationships that cause me to personally prefer local over online.

Whichever route you decide is right for your context, here are a few questions to ask and things to look for:

Price
Obviously you want to find the best quality for the lowest price. Just make sure you are comparing apples to apples when price shopping. Things often included in the price with one company might be add-ons for another company (premium paper, pre-flighting, binding, collating, delivery fees, etc.).

Minimum Quantities
Some printers will have minimum quantities for certain types of publications (500 business cards might be a minimum order, for example). Others give discounts at certain quantity tiers. If you order 10,000 weekly bulletins a month—and are willing to commit to ordering that many for six months—you can probably negotiate a discount with some printers.

Digital vs. Traditional

Some projects lend themselves better to printing on digital machines, others require traditional machines (think huge printing presses with mixed ink). Did you know letterhead has to be printed using traditional printing because of the type of ink required? Toner from a digital press would smear if run through an office copy machine or office printer.

It's nice when a printing company has both digital and traditional presses in house, but most do not. In those cases, your printer will have to outsource when they don't have the right type of machine.

Standard Turnaround Time

If you are going to need a quick turn-around, such as with a weekend bulletin, you need to factor that in to the printing company you choose.

File Formats & File Delivery Methods

The preferred method for receiving your file and the preferred file type and configuration will vary from printer to printer. If you do most of your designing in Photoshop, for example, you will want to make sure to find a printing company who can accept that file type and handle the large file size.

Some printers I've used had a web based file uploader. Some assigned me an FTP account. Others preferred I upload a file to my web server where they could get it.

These are all factors to consider in your selection process.

Designer On Staff

Sometimes you need a designer to lay out a publication for you. Though I am a designer myself, it was handy when the printing company had someone on staff who spoke the same language as me when talking printing. And if you're not a designer, it helps when the printer's staff can translate printer speak into English.

Extras

There are lots of "extra" features that printing companies can offer. A few examples include variable data, binding, special finishing effects like UV coating or die-cutting, etc. Ask prospective printers what extra options they offer for your print pieces.

Choosing a Ministry Partner

Ultimately, when choosing a printing company you are choosing a partnership. When a wise choice is made, a good relationship with them can make your life as a church staffer a lot easier. I recommend informally interviewing prospective companies, asking to tour the facilities and generally beginning a dialog.

Remember, as with any vendor you work with as a church organization, you don't want to be just another customer. You are representing Christ and will ultimately have the opportunity to do ministry as a result of this choice.

Chuck Scoggins is the owner of 374 Designs, coordinator of the CFCC Church Marketing Lab, author of the book, *Getting Started In Church Communications*, and part of the Creative Missions leadership team.

Web: ChuckScoggins.com
Twitter: @ChuckScoggins

HOW TO DO VIDEO ON A BUDGET
BY DAVE HARTLAND

I started doing video for my church 10 years ago. I used my own $300 handheld camcorder and edited it on my own computer using the cheapest video editing software I could find.

Ten years later I am now the full-time director of video at my church. I don't use a camcorder anymore. I have several high-end cameras and video editing software suites. My team produces several videos a week, including the sermon videos for our multisite locations.

Getting here hasn't been an easy road, nor has it been cheap. For those of you just starting your journey or for those without the means to purchase expensive equipment and software—fear not! It's not as overwhelming or as impossible as it may seem.

Make the Most of What You Have

Early on I had to learn to be content with a limited budget and equipment. I became real familiar with what I call the "Good Enough Principle." I would not be able to duplicate things I saw on TV using a handheld camcorder. I started out with iMovie and Windows MovieMaker, and eventually graduated to Final Cut Express. They weren't top of the line editing suites, but I still did everything I could to make our videos the best they could be with what we had.

Today you can shell out for high-end software or go

with cheap stuff. But I've learned it doesn't matter what software you use if you're producing a simple announcement or testimony video. What matters is what you have available in real life. I had a few people I could count on in front of a camera. We started producing things like sermon illustrations and eventually began to incorporate more of our service elements, such as announcements, into video. I worked with the creative and communications teams to get the artwork or graphics I needed for the projects. I knew that as long as I had the right people, and I was able to use the technology we had to add music or graphics, the videos would be good enough.

Continuing Education

Today's rapid-fire advances in technology can make a turkey look smarter than you if you don't keep up with the changes. Thankfully there's an endless supply of online resources that can keep you current on the latest techniques. Just search for tutorials, how-to guides and videos from websites such as Ken Rockwell (http://cmsucks.us/n7) and Ripple Training(http://cmsucks.us/n8). Set aside some dedicated time and never stop learning.

It's All About the Shot

One day last summer I was filming a sermon at the beach for our Jonah series. I did not realize until I began editing that there was a couple making out on the beach in the distance behind the pastor.

It doesn't matter if you're using a $5 editing program on your iPhone or a $2,500 pro editing suite on your souped up desktop. If the shot isn't set up correctly, there's very little you can do to salvage your project in post-production.

Make sure the camera is in focus, the subjects are well lit and ensure there are no obvious distractions in the shot, like the hum of an air conditioner or somebody in the background doing cartwheels. Not only will setting up your shot correctly help you in post-production, it will also enable you to give your audience a distraction-free production that will enlighten, teach, inform and inspire.

Wrapping It Up in a Neat Little Bow
A well-made video needs to pique the interest of those watching it. That means adding text, graphics and music to the final product. Again, you don't need an expensive piece of software to create something good. There are loads of resources on the Internet for you to utilize. A couple quick suggestions:

- Video Blocks (http://cmsucks.us/n9) is a great tool that will give you unlimited downloads of thousands of sound effects, production music, motion backgrounds and video clips for only $79 per month.
- CreationSwap (http://cmsucks.us/n3) has been a great resource for graphics and backgrounds.
- Freeplay Music (http://cmsucks.us/na) has an endless library of production music. Other music resources include Incompetech (http://cmsucks.us/nb) and Free Music Archive (http://cmsucks.us/nc).

Another "free" way of obtaining music for your video—if you have the capability to do so—is having your worship leader record something for you that matches the video's mood. It's amazing what music and graphics can do to spice up an otherwise boring video.

Everybody Has a Story to Tell

Perhaps the most important aspect of a video ministry is helping tell God's story. There is nothing more powerful than a well-told story about someone whose life has been changed by Jesus. Fortunately, God's story can be told with or without money or expensive equipment. So even if you're working with a handheld camcorder and a flashlight, just turn the camera on, have the subject tell their story, add some soft piano music in the background and let God do the rest. That story has the potential to change lives. We pray that hearts are moved to worship Jesus through their story.

Video Samples

Here are some simple videos made during past Creative Missions trips to show what can be done quickly and simply:

- River of Life Church – Albany, N.Y. (http://cmsucks.us/ne)
- Boundless Grace Baptist Church – Avoca, Ark. (http://cmsucks.us/nf)
- Metro Church – Rogers, Ark. (http://cmsucks.us/ng)
- Beaver Lake Baptist Church – Beaver Lake, Ark. (http://cmsucks.us/nd)

Dave Hartland is the director of video ministries at Grace Church in Erie, Pa. He loves snow, traveling and tea.

Twitter: @DaveHartland

SIMPLE TWEAKS TO IMPROVE YOUR SOUND SYSTEM

BY COLT MELROSE

Every church has a sound system, right? Even if you are a church plant, one of the first things you bought was probably a sound system. But just because you have a sound system doesn't mean you know how to best utilize it. So let's look at some simple fixes to make your sound system rock.

What Can You Turn Down?
We all have that vocalist who complains about not being able to hear their own voice, so we turn them up. Then the keyboard player can't hear the bass, so we turn it up. Then... well, you get the point.

Instead of always turning something up, find ways to turn other things down. Once you find the balance between your instruments and vocals, you can adjust the master volume to a comfortable level for the room.

As much as possible, reduce the stage volume. This would include amps for the guitars, monitors and louder acoustic instruments like drums or piano. This is especially important for smaller spaces. When the stage volume is too loud, it forces the main levels up, which reduces comfort and clarity in your auditorium.

What About the Drums?
If you have drums you need a solid kick/snare presence to support the rest of the players, but it doesn't have to give you a heart attack on every downbeat. Find a way to control the drum volume as much as possible, wheth-

er that's an enclosure for an acoustic kit or an electronic kit. Even if you can't fully enclose the drums, try a drum shield and a fabric backdrop. The more you can contain the drums, the more you can control your mix.

Identify Your Musical Hierarchy

When you build your mix, start with the kick/snare and set a solid bottom. Then identify which instrument is going to lead the congregation and bring it to the front. Then just fill in with everyone else from there.

This is also true for vocals. While your vocal levels should always be just above the instruments, it is best to identify who is going to lead the vocal team on the platform. They should be the most identifiable voice.

Understand Your Console

If you are the audio engineer (aka "Sound Guy"), chances are you are a volunteer. You likely don't have any training, or the small amount of training you received was from the guy who installed the system and it lasted about 20 minutes.

Take the time and responsibility to learn how to effectively use the EQ system, auxiliary sends and buses as well as any effects processors like reverb. The Internet is full of tutorials. Invest the time to understand what all those knobs and sliders do and how they work best.

If you can afford it, hire a local freelance audio engineer to come spend a few hours with your volunteer team during a rehearsal and give some on-site training.

Colt Melrose is the media pastor at Parkway Fellowship in Katy, Texas. He is a volunteer-turned-pastor who has served local churches in Oklahoma, Indiana and Texas for the past 14 years.

Facebook: /ColtMelrose
Twitter: @ColtMelrose

HOW TO WRITE CHURCH ANNOUNCEMENTS

BY KELVIN CO

Regardless of the size, worship style or technology use of your church, writing announcements is a vital communication function. And because department heads or ministry leaders tend to either give you too much or not enough information to promote their event, writing announcements is a chronically challenging task.

People typically try to make announcements sound as exciting as possible by embellishing them with as many adjectives and adverbs as they can. I did. The resulting copy usually ends up being a difficult to navigate set of churchy dribble.

Here's an example:

> If you are married or planning to get married the Renewed Marriage Seminar is for you and your spouse. Join our senior pastor and his wife, John and Jane Smith, for this incredible time of renewal and refreshing in your marriage. Having been married 20 years, they will be teaching marriage principles from the Bible as well as from their own experiences. The registration fee is $35, which includes study materials, lunch and snacks. Childcare will be provided. The seminar is on March 9 from 10 a.m. to 2 p.m. The seminar will be in the fellowship hall. Lunch and refreshments will be served in the atrium. Register at the table in the atrium after the service or call Dorothy at the church office.

Compounded with the rest of the churchy dribble in the bulletin, it all becomes noise that collectively screams, "Ignore me!"

A Better Way

I am not a gifted writer. It takes me longer than most people to organize thoughts into words. Considering the volume of announcements and how much energy and time it takes to manage and write them, I had to figure out a way to do it more effectively and efficiently. I developed a basic format/template that not only simplified the process but has made our announcements significantly more clear and meaningful. Using the above example, this is how the announcement would look after applying my template:

> Renewed Marriage Seminar // Saturday, March 9, 10 a.m. to 2 p.m. // Fellowship Hall // Pastor John and Jane Smith will teach marriage principles from the Bible and their own experience. Register ($35 includes materials, lunch and childcare) in the atrium or by contacting Dorothy (555-555-1234 or dorothy@church.org).

Some key thoughts behind this format:

- Placing the what, when and where upfront makes it easy for people to find key information they need to know as opposed to navigating through sentences to figure out the basic information about an event.
- This format shaved off significant time in writing copy for me.
- It streamlined the communication process of capturing the information needed to promote events from announcement requesters.
- Putting the day of the week before the date is a good rule to follow. It is easier for people to make scheduling decisions when they know what day of the week an event is.

- The main purpose of announcements is to get someone to respond to the opportunity. Stating the call-to-action clearly is a must.

This is one of the simplest free solutions I implemented with optimal pay off. Hope it works for you.

> Kelvin Co gets to do what he loves as the creative arts pastor of The Oaks Fellowship located in the Dallas Metroplex area. Kelvin has been doing life together with his wife and best friend Lucy since 1991 and together they've been doting and pouring into their son Luc since 2002.

Web: KelvinCo.com
Twitter: @KelvinCo

TOP 5 ELEMENTS FOR A CHURCH SITE
BY MATT ADAMS

All church websites need to clearly address these five basic questions: Who, what, when, where and how.

Easy, huh?

Who

Who are you? Your church name, leadership and mission should be clear. Introduce the key leaders and staff members. For a first time guest, it's comforting to see what the pastor looks like and recognize a few staff members. Especially when they need help, directions or have questions.

What

What do you stand for, what is your church doing to communicate the love of Jesus? Share your projects and outreach ministries in an easy to browse format. Make sure your mission, vision and theology are clear. Don't make a visitor hunt for any of this information.

When

When do you meet? My family recently moved to a new city and needed to hunt for a new church. I was floored by how hard this was on many of the church sites we browsed. Could be great churches, but they never stood a chance in my book. We had about 10 churches on our short list and half were dropped pretty quickly due to the lack of information. Sure we could have called or emailed, but half the churches on our list had clear info. Once we found the church we liked, we stopped the search.

Don't expect your users to reach out if they can't find the service times. They will simply move on.

Where

Just as important as when you meet is where you meet. For some brick and mortar churches this is less difficult than a mobile/portable church. Regardless, sharing your address is just the tip of the iceberg.

Communicate the best directions, parking, children's check in, etc. Anything possible to ease the first five minutes of your guest experience will go a long way with any visitor.

How

How can someone get engaged with the church? Events, ministries, missions, service, etc. This is secondary information to the above. Keep in mind the person looking for this info has likely been to your church a few times, but a new visitor will still want to see this info even if they don't engage yet. It communicates how you are living out your mission and vision.

Provide points of engagement and action on all these pages. Promote these internally to get church members to sign up, connect with a ministry leader, and volunteer. Don't forget to close the loop with a call to action!

Bonus Tip: Make it Accessible.

Everything you do online needs to be mobile friendly. It's estimated that 50% of all consumer traffic this year will be on a touch device. iPads, Android tablets, smart phones—we all have one or two. While being mobile responsive is my personal goal on every site, just being mobile friendly will suffice for this list. No flash, no crazy scripts that can crash and avoid text in images.

Final Take Away

Keep all the above in mind first and foremost as you're working on your website. Clear information and ease of use will go further than flashy graphics. Keep it simple and usable.

Matt Adams is a full-time web designer for factor1, a digital creative agency located in Tempe, Ariz. He and his wife have twin boys and spend more hours cycling than most sane people can imagine.

Web: factor1studios.com
Twitter: @mattada

HOW TO FIND A WEB COMPANY FOR YOUR CHURCH

BY MATT ADAMS

Here you are, finally with a budget and senior staff sign off on building your church a new website. How exciting! Seriously, it probably took months, maybe years to get here. Now you need to start ironing out who you are going to use and how they will build the site of your dreams, in your budget and with your brand in mind.

Narrow Your Results

First off, know your budget. Do you have $2,000 to spend or $10,000? These are vastly different site developers. Don't kick the tires of the $10,000 companies hoping they will have a special price for you. You're wasting their time and yours. If the company doesn't showcase their pricing front and center, or at least offer some sort of range, present your budget in the quote request. Let them know you have $4,000-$5,000 to spend. Or $500 to spend. If they can't help you, hopefully they will let you know right away and point you in some other direction.

Check out the Church Marketing Sucks resources (http://cmsucks.us/nh) and ask around. The Church Marketing Lab (http://cmsucks.us/ni) is a great place to have conversations with other church communication pros. Also look around at other churches, nonprofits and business sites you like and find out who built them.

Portfolios

Look at portfolios, but don't stop there. All web developers put their best work up front, and some include work that isn't the final production site. Google the company name, and see some of their other work. Keep in mind with both the good and the bad, the content is usually not their doing. So pink Comic Sans on the kids' ministry graphic or the amazing 3D sermon series artwork are often the product of a site admin and church staff/volunteer.

Know Your Needs

Mobile responsive? Blogs? Sermon media grids? The more you know your content, styles and key deliverables, the better you can direct the proposal and the project. It's so much easier to get all the constraints, needs and known facts on the table upfront. Surprises in construction of anything cost time and money.

Template or Custom?

Know what you need and want. For some, this may be a function of your budget. Not everyone needs to re-invent the wheel, but for me personally, I have never been to a church just like any other in brand, style, demographics or culture. So it's tough to see a template with a dropped in brand being a great fit.

Who Will Manage the Site?

When it's all done and live, who updates the content, images and podcasts? Someone with some basic web and Photoshop skills? Or the church secretary who knows Word? This can help the web design company plan and coordinate the training and construction to make the site a good fit.

Write a Brief

Outline all of the above items in a clear-cut, one-page

document. Share this with web companies as early in the process as you can. Albert Einstein once said if you can not explain it quickly, you don't understand it well enough. Download a sample brief as well as a blank brief in PDF and a Word doc at http://cmsucks.us/mm.

Review the Proposals

Hopefully your brief will keep the proposals in the same league, and you can compare apples to apples. Review upfront costs, as well as ongoing costs. Many companies will have monthly server costs. Often this is just hosting, say $15-$30 a month. But others may charge upwards of $100 a month.

Know Who Owns It

Do you own the site or are you just borrowing it? I know some pretty big (but talented) companies that bill $2,000-8,000, in addition to $100 or more a month, and the church is just leasing the site, with no access to the code or any ability to move the finished site to another host. This works for some people, but keep it in mind when comparing proposals.

Matt Adams is a full-time web designer for factor1, a digital creative agency located in Tempe, Ariz. He and his wife have twin boys and spend more hours cycling than most sane people can imagine.

Web: factor1studios.com
Twitter: @mattada

GETTING ORGANIZED WITH GOOGLE

BY EVAN COURTNEY

Google has several tools churches can leverage to effectively communicate internally and externally to their communities. These tools allow for creative collaboration and the ability to share with multiple users.

How to Get Started
1. Create a church specific Google Account that will be the ultimate owner of everything and will create key documents. Creating a church account as opposed to using an individual account will make staff transitions easier.
2. Share documents, spreadsheets, forms and calendars with the appropriate staff, assigning them privileges to view and/or edit as needed.
3. Start adding content.

Google Docs

There are several major advantages to Google Docs: They're free, they're stored in the cloud so you can access documents anywhere and they offer excellent collaboration tools. But another big plus for churches is the ability to share documents, either publicly or with select people.

How can your church start using it today?

- Create shared folders for different ministries and new documents can be automatically shared with everyone on the team.

- Share important internal documents like style guides and be able to keep them current without having to distribute updated versions.

- Make important documents public, like financial disclosures, safe church policies, job descriptions and more. This is especially helpful for documents that will be updated frequently but you don't want to mess with updating and uploading a PDF.

Google Spreadsheets

Google Spreadsheets work very similar to Microsoft Excel or Apple Numbers, but are stored in the cloud and allow for multiple collaborators. Also they have a great notifications feature that will email you with individual updates or a daily summary.

How can your church start using it today?
Organize and sort data collected from visitor cards, communications cards, etc. Multiple staff are then able to view and edit the spreadsheet.

Google Forms

This Google application gives churches the ability to accept data from a form and put it into a spreadsheet.

How can your church start using it today?

- Event registration - This can only be used for free events, since Google Forms doesn't accept payments. If you need paid event registration try Wufoo.

- On site registration - A great option instead of paper registration that requires time-consuming data entry

and deciphering illegible handwriting. A great use would be Easter Egg Hunts, Fall Festivals, etc.
- Sign up sheet - Phil Schneider's church is using it on Sundays for people to sign up for events instead of the old clipboard.
- Communication requests - Ministries can easily submit their communication/marketing needs.

Google Calendar

This is a powerful tool that can keep the church calendar organized and make it easy to publish to websites and share with the church. You can create as many calendars as you want, but it's easy to make it too complicated. I recommend keeping it simple with an internal and external calendar. The pastors at our church then have their own individual calendars for ministry appointments that are shared among themselves and admin assistants.

Internal calendar: Create a private calendar to share with and be edited by all staff. This is a good way to communicate about internal events among the staff and key volunteers. Typical uses:

- Facility use
- Staff vacation days
- Non-public events/dates (i.e., staff meeting, staff prayer, sermon planning, committee meetings, etc.)
- When someone is out of the office

External calendar: Create a calendar to share publicly, but only the communications department or ministry heads can edit it. This is a good way to broadcast dates to the church and community. Typical uses:

- Worship service times
- Any and all church events

Each event on the calendar should have minimal information—time, date and location—and a URL linking to a corresponding web page or Facebook event with a more detailed description (you don't want to update information in multiple places).

Sharing Your External Calendar
Share your public calendar to get the most out of Google Calendar:

1. Subscribe: You'll want to share the RSS feed and iCal link so users can subscribe and add it to their own calendar. Now your congregation can have all the upcoming church events on their favorite device.
2. Embed: Add your calendar to your website or blog.
3. Help: Offer your congregation some pointers for using Google Calendar. Show them how to use color coding, set reminders and sync their devices.

Get Organized
Google offers a lot of great services to keep you organized and they're constantly rolling out new stuff and new features. But don't forget that things are always changing—remember Google Reader?—enjoy these tools while you can. Experiment and find out what works for you.

Evan Courtney is a family life pastor and communications director in the middle of the cornfields of Illinois at The Fields Church. He's a graphic designer, media consultant and eBay PowerSeller.

Web: EvanCourtney.com
Twitter: @EvanCourtney

GETTING YOUR CHURCH STARTED WITH FACEBOOK

BY MATT ADAMS

Facebook is beyond popular. Over 1 billion people are registered to use the social media giant as of September 2012. With that many people on Facebook, it's a perfect place to have your church be active, alive and interacting with users. Facebook is super easy to use and easy to get started.

Maybe you already have a Facebook fan page for your church and it needs to be dusted off, or maybe it's a new idea and you don't know where to start. Either way, we can help your church get started on Facebook.

How to Create a Page

First off, you need to create a page for your church. So log in to your Facebook account. (Don't have an account? Time to join 1 billion others.)

Visit facebook.com/pages to create your church's page. Choose to create a page for a Company, Organization or Institution. This is best for most churches. Then select Church/Religious Organization. Now simply follow the next few steps to fill in the details about your church.

Page URL

Make sure you set your Facebook web address. This will make it easier for people to find your church on Facebook. Pick something short and simple, but clear. Facebook won't let you change this URL, so be sure it's the best choice. (While the form says you can't change it, Facebook's Help Center says they'll let you change it once. Either way, be sure.)

Already on Facebook but have that ugly string of numbers for your URL? Here's a fix for that: facbook.com/username. You can set a custom username for any person or organization you administer.

Key Elements

There are a few key things you need to work on with Facebook:

1. Set a good profile image. Use your logo, but make sure it's readable at different sizes. The profile image is square, so plan accordingly.
2. Keep your cover photo (the big banner on top) up to date. Using current sermon series/event artwork is great. The Facebook cover photo is 851 pixels wide by 315 pixels tall, and your profile photo sits in the lower left, covering a small portion, so be conscious of that.

How to Connect Your Site to Your New Page

Facebook has a few great tools for you to add "like" buttons and share buttons to your website. These are little bits of code, but it's pretty much a copy and paste deal, so if you are slightly web savvy, you should be OK. But don't hesitate to ask a pro to do this for you.

You can check out the full set of social plugins, but the Like Button is one you really want to use. It allows users to like your Facebook page from your website and gives them the option to share with their friends. There's a form to fill out that will generate your code.

Leave the 'URL to like' field blank if you're adding this code to every page on your site. Tinker with the options to see what fits your site best.

Get Help

Facebook pages allow for multiple administrators, so get some. This is good for accountability, but also good practice. You can spread out the responsibility and not force one person to do all the work. Plus, if someone on the admin team quits, gets fired or is asked to no longer volunteer, you need to remove them from the admin roles ASAP.

A current admin can add new admins from the Admin Panel, assigning different levels of control and access.

Keep Trying

You can do a lot with Facebook and it's constantly evolving, so keep experimenting. Hopefully these tips will get your church started. Once you're up and running, check out ways to get better at Facebook and learn how to get lots of likes.

Matt Adams is a full-time web designer for factor1, a digital creative agency located in Tempe, Ariz. He and his wife have twin boys and spend more hours cycling than most sane people can imagine.

Web: factor1studios.com
Twitter: @mattada

7 THINGS EVERY CHURCH FACEBOOK EXPERT SHOULD KNOW

BY CLEVE PERSINGER

No matter where you're at in the Facebook process at your church, knowing these seven things will immediately make you smarter and impress others as you defend your Facebook expert status.

1. Just Jump In!

A lot of pastors and ministry leaders think they have to have Facebook all figured out before they create a page. Some even read books about it. I keep waiting to hear about churches organizing Facebook committees.

My advice? Just jump in! Stop waiting to get your Facebook ducks in a row. The beauty of social media is it's so new and ever-changing you'll be an "expert" after a little time and some trial and error.

2. It's Not a Fad

Some ask before they invest their time learning Facebook, "How long until the next fad comes around?" Don't dwell on that. Nothing lasts forever, but you can take advantage of Facebook's good run.

I only visit my church's website once every day, but I visit Facebook constantly through desktop and mobile. Facebook is where people are. Consider these recent stats:

- 93% of U.S. adult Internet users are on Facebook. 70% are active daily.

- The majority of Facebook users are ages 18 to 55.
- Users spend 10.5 billion minutes on Facebook daily.

3. It's Strategic

Your church building isn't the only place where church happens. You send your members out into the community. Likewise your church website isn't the only place to be online.

Don't let your church website be the only place folks can find out about what's going on. Facebook should be an online representation of your church where folks get to know each other and keep up with what's happening in the life of your church.

4. Posting Tips

There are no perfect formulas for Facebook, but these best practices will set you up for success.

Find Your Rhythm

Facebook says the best times to post are 8:00 a.m., 11:00 a.m., 2:00 p.m. and 8:00 p.m. When can people expect updates on your page? I suggest posting at least once a day. Consider developing a posting strategy and schedule posts ahead of time with free tools like HootSuite (http://cmsucks.us/nj) and BufferApp (http://cmsucks.us/nk) or directly on Facebook.

Videos and Images

Add a face to your church. Show life and changed lives inside your church. Posts that include a video get an average of 100% more interaction, and images 120%.

That contraption in your pocket is a camera and video camera. Use it! Some examples include:

- Sermon videos.
- Weekly pastor webcam video: "Here's what God is teaching me."
- Testimony videos: Changed lives change lives.
- Weekend reporting: Live stills of the pastor preaching or sermon slides
- Celebrate baptisms!
- Gatherings and event photos: Tag people and then their friends see it.
- Inspirational images with Bible verses or quotes are popular. Two great sites to grab images from are Pinterest and CreationSwap (http://cmsucks.us/n3).

Short = Better
The shorter status updates get my attention. Posts fewer than three lines of text or between 100-150 characters see 60% more likes, comments and shares than longer posts. It's kind of like billboards.

Engage
Put the bullhorn away and start a two-way conversation.

- Make sure your page has more question marks than periods (see http://cmsucks.us/bi).
- Fill-in-the-blank posts generate about 90% more interaction.
- Encourage folks on Friday to read the passage

you're covering on the weekend and then ask them on Monday what God taught them.

Add Value
Does your content add value? Do people want to share it? Would you want to share it with your friends and family? Reach out beyond the walls of your Facebook page but still point back to it.

High Fives and Hurts
Publically high-five volunteers through Facebook. Post their picture and tag them.

Pastors who grasp the power of Facebook realize it's about rejoicing with folks who are rejoicing and hurting with those who are hurting. They use Facebook to get to know their flock and meet them where they are.

5. Recruit Volunteers
If successful, it's going to turn into a big job. Who can you recruit to help you post and respond? What specifically do you want them to post? Sometimes these volunteers will be apparent based on their comment frequency and quality on your page. I've heard of several stay-at-home moms who really rock this volunteer role and didn't realize it was a legit way to volunteer at church beforehand.

6. Spread the Word
Make sure you have a good Facebook web address (facebook.com/yourname) and spread the word. Like your web address, it should be easy to find. Include it on church communication just like you would the web address. Some churches even get the word out by print-

ing their Facebook address on giveaways like blue pens.

7. Read About It

Since Facebook is constantly evolving, continuing your education and knowledge is key to staying relevant with your church's Facebook strategy. Look at other church Facebook pages for inspiration and read blogs that cover the topic. Here are several resources that will keep you in the know:

- ChurchMarketingSucks.com
- MediaBleep.com
- ChurchJuice.com
- PhilBowdle.com

Cleve Persinger helps churches engage community both online and off. He's the external communications strategist for The Chapel, a multi-site church in Chicagoland, and founder of MediaBLEEP and Creative Missions.

Web: MediaBLEEP.com
Twitter: @persinger

4 MISTAKES FROM MY FIRST 3 YEARS AS A COMMUNICATIONS DIRECTOR

BY PHIL BOWDLE

March 2013 marked my three-year anniversary as communications director at West Ridge Church. It has been an incredible blessing to work for a church that I love, respect and would choose to attend.

These three years have been filled with triumphs, challenges, loss and lessons. I still have a long way to go, but I've learned a lot about myself and the role of communication in the church. Looking back specifically on my role as communications director, here are four mistakes from my first three years in this role as well as some lessons I've learned along the way.

1. I didn't have a focused volunteer strategy.

Getting qualified and consistent volunteers engaged in a church communications team can be very challenging. At first, I would attempt to get anyone interested plugged in, no matter their level of talent or time available. I didn't spend the time upfront building solid job descriptions for each position with qualifications and the required time commitment. Because I didn't communicate proper expectations, people got lost in the shuffle. In the second year, I refocused my volunteer strategy with higher expectations for time and qualifications, and then dedicated more time to investing and equipping volunteers.

Lesson: Start with simple volunteer job descriptions

with qualifications and expectations for each volunteer position. It's OK to have high expectations for talent and time commitment as long as it's communicated upfront.

2. I didn't set a healthy and sustainable pace.

Coming into my role as communications director, I knew I was building something from the ground up. There wasn't an established team or systems in place to build from. I was doing the building. Luckily, that's exactly what I love to do!

The challenge was that the needs and demands exceeded what I could do in a 40-hour workweek. Almost every day I'd find myself waking up early or staying up late trying to get caught up, only to find myself never getting there. This pressure was by no means coming from my boss (quite the opposite), but more from how I'm wired. I'm always thinking about what's next and how can we take what we're doing to the next level. The pace was not healthy or sustainable for me. To be honest, I still struggle with this. This is a constant tension to manage.

Lesson: Focus from the beginning on creating a healthy and sustainable pace for what you're doing. You can't do everything overnight. Focus on the critical needs, identify the non-critical needs and attack them over the year strategically so you and your team are being healthy and sustainable. Schedule vacation time at the beginning of the year. It's a marathon, not a sprint.

3. I was too slow to make our website mobile.

In the first year, we rebuilt WestRidge.com from the ground up with brand new content and a new content management system (Expression Engine). Our web traffic has grown steadily since then as we've built a trust with our audience that our site is the number one place to find the information they need.

What I underestimated in the first two years was how quickly mobile traffic would grow. Just last year, over one-third of our traffic (almost 80,000 visits) came from mobile. So at the end of 2012, we rebuilt our site to be responsive so it's now mobile friendly and works well on all desktop and mobile platforms. The results and traffic growth have been fantastic. I just wish we had done it sooner.

Lesson: If you're redesigning your website, make sure it is responsive and mobile friendly. If your site is not currently mobile friendly, start making plans now to make that change.

4. I let long-term vision get lost in short-term tasks.

Too many times in my first three years I would get caught in a reactionary workflow and spend much of my time answering emails, putting out fires and responding to short-term tasks. My mistake was that I didn't block out time to dream and evaluate where we were as a team and build a vision for where we needed to go. Without realizing it, I was sacrificing the long-term vision for the short-term needs.

Lesson: Schedule time at least once a month to sit back and evaluate where you are and where you and your team need to be. It's always going to be busy, but this time is crucial for your leadership. Block off some time monthly to build a plan and vision for the future.

Overseeing communication for your church is a difficult job, even for those of us doing it full time. I hope these lessons offer some insight and perspective. Improving how your church communicates can make you dangerous, but not bulletproof. We can always learn from our mistakes.

Phil Bowdle is the communications director at West Ridge Church in Atlanta. You can follow along with his blog at PhilBowdle.com, which is focused on being a practical conversation and resource on church communications.

Web: PhilBowdle.com
Twitter: @PhilBowdle

NEED MORE?

Outspoken: Conversations on Church Communication

The church has the greatest story ever told: the message of the gospel. Unfortunately, most churches aren't doing a great job of communicating it. The way the world communicates has changed dramatically in recent years. With the rise of the web and social media, many churches are in the dark about where to go or what to do next.

Drawing on the wisdom and insight from over 60 leading experts in various fields of church communication, this book provides a comprehensive resource for church leaders sharing how the church can leverage new media to effectively connect people with the gospel.

From branding and design, to websites and social media, there are endless ways your church can cut through the static and help the message of the gospel be heard clearly.

We've got a message worth sharing. It's time we learn how to communicate it and communicate it well.

It's time to be outspoken!

Outspoken: Conversations on Church Communication is available from Amazon in print and digital formats.

ABOUT THE CENTER FOR CHURCH COMMUNICATION

We are a firebrand of communicators, sparking churches to communicate the gospel clearly, effectively and without compromise.

We are made up of passionate change agents, experienced communication professionals and thoughtful instigators; advocating for communicators to find their place in the church—and helping the church get through to their communities so that churches know who they are and are unashamed to tell others.

We identify, resource and celebrate the next generation of church communicators, encouraging them to focus their tenacity and talent for excellent communication, so that churches are sought out by the communities they serve.

We provide smart coaching and mentoring through social media, publishing, events and one-on-one relationships, spotlighting communication that is true, good and beautiful—prompting others to do the same—so that more outsiders become a part of a church community.

We remove barriers to change the way people see Christians and how they speak about the church by promoting relationships, resources, ideas and models for communication. We collaborate people's gifts/skills to work in concert with the Creator and their local church.

As God's story comes alive to us and others, we see gospel-centered local churches that captivate the attention and liberate the imagination of their community, resulting in more people saying, **"That's what church should be!"**

Center for Church Communication:
Courageous storytellers welcome.
CFCCLabs.org

Check out some of our projects:

Church Marketing Sucks
http://churchmarketingsucks.com
The blog to frustrate, educate and motivate the church to communicate, with uncompromising clarity, the truth of Jesus Christ.

Church Marketing Lab
http://cfcclabs.org/cml
Show your work, share your feedback.

Job Board
http://jobs.cfcclabs.org/
Find or complete the winning team.

Freelance Board
http://freelance.cfcclabs.org/
Find or freelance your next project.

Church Marketing Directory
http://directory.cfcclabs.org/
Tools, resources and companies that help the church communicate better.

Firestarter
http://cfcclabs.org/firestarter
Celebrating churches that have sparked brilliant communication.

Local Labs
http://cfcclabs.org/local
Meet up with fellow church communicators.

Events Calendar
http://cfcclabs.org/events
Church communication related events.

ABOUT CREATIVE MISSIONS

Creative Missions is a missions trip where church creatives can put the skills God has given them to use by helping churches communicate better.

Jon Rogers, who has served on several trips, said it well:

> "No, we didn't build a church building or construct an orphanage. No, we didn't run a VBS or witness on the streets. We created sustainable solutions for churches to effectively communicate an ultimate message of God's never-ending love for each community these churches are involved in."

Each year a team of church communication professionals travels to a specific area and serves a collection of local churches. In 2011 it was Albany, N.Y. In 2012 it was Northwest Arkansas and Joplin, Mo. In 2013 it was Anchorage, Alaska.

The Gospel Purpose

"Many first time guests have said they came as a result of the work that you did," said Anthony Foxworth of River Albany Church.

That's the idea: To help churches communicate better so they can be more effective in their communities. Like any other missionary, the goal is to spread the gospel. But Creative Missions does it with websites, videos and communication strategy, instead of painting, kids programs or street teams.

Needed Encouragement
"This week has lifted a huge weight off my shoulders as a lead pastor," said Andy Swart of Metro Church.

It's a shot in the arm for local pastors. The Creative Missions team tackles tasks these pastors were ill-equipped to handle, projects that were simply weighing them down. All by lending an ear and a helping hand.

"You know why I like you guys?" asked Darrin Smith of Journey Church. "You listen to me."

Helping the Helpers
Like any good missions trip, the missionaries themselves are also changed:

"Coming into this trip, I was feeling inadequate at best and very insecure," said Kyna Moore, a photographer, videographer and Creative Missions veteran. "I'm so thankful I was able to come and I really am leaving feeling refreshed and rejuvenated, despite the long days."

The creative and tech gurus learn lessons and insights of their own as they work closely (and feverishly!) with other professionals over the week of the trip. Iron sharpens iron, and these communicators return home better at what they do and inspired to do more.

Founded by Cleve Persinger with the help of Eric Murrell and Andy Burns, Creative Missions exists thanks to the support of countless donors and sponsors. Creative Missions also works in partnership with the Center for

Church Communication, which champions the effort and handles the finances. Finally, Creative Missions wouldn't exist without the dozens of volunteers who sacrifice a week of vacation each year to share their skills and help churches communicate better.

To learn more about Creative Missions visit http://creativemissions.to

ACKNOWLEDGMENTS

Thanks to Cleve Persinger, Chuck Scoggins, Kevin D. Hendricks and Laura Bennett for pulling this book together.

Big thanks to our contributors: Matt Adams, Laura Bennett, Phil Bowdle, Kelvin Co, Evan Courtney, Kim Fukai, Danielle Hartland, Dave Hartland, Kevin D. Hendricks, Colt Melrose, Eric Murrell, Cleve Persinger, Joe Porter and Chuck Scoggins.

Thanks to everybody who makes Creative Missions happen.

Thanks to the pastors and communicators struggling to tell courageous stories. You're not alone.

Thank you for reading this book. If you found it valuable, we hope you'll spread the word.

Made in the USA
Lexington, KY
17 June 2013